KU-348-854

WINTER BREAKS

Gordon Hodgeon

Smoke
STACK
BOOKS

821.914

0045294135

To Alice, Bernie, Daniel, Julia & Robbie

'so young beasts thrive'

'We all, those of us without the comforts of religion and no doubt many who sincerely believe themselves to be religious, live our lives according to our own selected fictions. The centre of mine is about the importance of going on going on. 'Stoically' would be too large a word: 'stubbornly' will be better, sometimes perkily and cheerfully, sometimes grumpily.'

Richard Hoggart, *An Imagined Life – Life and Times 1959-91*

'The iron shoes I wore for thee,
the mountain of ice I clamb for thee.'

from 'The Black Bull of Norroway,' quoted by Kathleen Raine in *The Land Unknown*

Acknowledgements

Acknowledgements are due to the editors of the following publications in which some of these poems first appeared: *Kenaz, Penniless Press*, Cynthia Fuller & Kevin Cadwallender (eds) *Smelter* (Mudfog, 2003), Subhadassi (sel) *The sensitively thin bill of the shag* (Biscuit, 2003), Maureen Almond (sel) *Challenges* (Biscuit, 2005), Cynthia Fuller & Andy Croft (eds) *North By North East* (IRON Press, 2006).

'The Price You Pay', then titled 'Cycling To The Rainbow', won the first Mirehouse Poetry Prize, Keswick, 2004.

Alongside the continuing debt to several dear friends, a close, patient and discerning readership, particular thanks with regard to these poems are due to Cynthia Fuller, Mandy Sutter, Bob McKee, Brotton Writers' Workshop and Hall Garth Poets for advice, ideas, encouragement and, sometimes, inspiration.

Published 2006
by

Smokestack Books
PO Box 408, Middlesbrough TS5 6WA
e-mail : info@smokestack-books.co.uk
www.smokestack-books.co.uk

Gordon Hodgeon © 2006
All rights reserved

Cover design by James Cianciaruso

Printed by
EPW Print & Design Ltd

ISBN 0-9551061-5-X
ISBN 978-0-9551061-5-6

Smokestack Books
gratefully acknowledges the support of
Middlesbrough Borough Council
and Arts Council North East

Smokestack Books is a member of
Independent Northern Publishers
www.northernpublishers.co.uk
and is represented by Inpress Ltd
www.inpressbooks.co.uk

Contents

The Baker   9

The Strap   11

Martha   12

The Woods   14

The Superintendent   17

Conspiratorial   19

How Are You Now?   20

Souvenirs   22

A Place To Write   23

Winter Breaks

1. Leaving   24

2. Severe   26

3. Hopeless Case   27

4. Likeness   28

5. Funereal   29

6. Restoration   31

7. Warming   32

8. Disposal   33

9. Recall   34

10. Notice   35

11. Zero   37

12. Circular   38

13. Freeze   40

14. Stuff   41

15. Collection   43

16. Accommodation   44

17. Liberty : A Letter   45

18. Soap   47

19. Waiting   49

20. Rambler   50

21. Call   51

22. Resolve   52

23. Love Song   53

24. Stranger   55

Inventing the Tenses   57

Viewer   58

Reading Your Spine   59

Tomb Decoration: Cattle   60

Song for Mario   61

This Once   62

In the Purse   64

Sunday Morning, Reading Drabble   65

Manhattan Piece   67

The Afternoon Slot   68

Early June 2003, Grandchildren   69

Beethoven Back of Blencarn   71

The Price You Pay   73

At St. Leonard's   74

No Ice   76

April in Coach B   78

Hand   79

Calvary   81

The Man In The Pub Said   82

February   83

Enquiry   84

Remains   85

Old Friend   86

Resolution   88

Lost Child   89

Old Wolves   90

Equinoctial   92

The Baker

I learned not to believe a word he said.
It didn't always work, but they're like that,
granddads, not quite grown up yet, not quite
playing the rules, not quite to be trusted.

The one I had lived in a baker's shop,
he was the baker, sold his backyard bread
in the downstairs front-room, buttered it
with Woodbines, Mint Imperials, bottled pop.

He let this grandson wander everywhere,
scullery, kitchen, landing. I could go
in the front parlour, play with the piano,
enter the shop, steal from the toffee jar.

In the long baking shed that filled the yard
were dusty sacks to sift white fingers in,
gas griddles quiet, waiting for the sign
to lift crisp muffins from the flour and lard.

But not the cellar. Dangerous, he warned,
catching me once too often at the sneck,
creaking the door ajar, sniffing the dark,
its pungent pool that lapped the top step's land.

'Why is it dangerous, Granddad?' 'Because,
my lad, of lack of light, the steep drop down,
the dead chap underneath his chiselled stone
in the flagged floor, and still one more because:

the well, just covered with a broken door,
so deep it could go down to endless night.'
I had to see all that, Jack Shiney-Light
and Granddad guiding the black-out tour.

I don't recall much else of that descent,
perhaps a smell of timber-damp, brick-mould,
a rusty hook that scratched, thick webs that fold
over the eyes, shadows that bent and bend

fifty years on to shroud me. A body,
was there, under that lettered stone? A well?
Never got down again, so I can't tell
the truth from tales with that old Methody.

I see now, in that dark, ghosts fetched from France.
Those dusty heaps are stockpiled newly dead
or sacks of loaves his kitchen cannot feed
to no-more-hungry mouths, wanting the chance

that limped him home, the shrapnel in his spine,
alive, to wife and son, chapel and shop
below which we two started on our drop
down planking steps into that sea-coal-mine

of our imaginings, while all around
and under us real pitmen bent and cut
and propped their tunnelling through fossil dirt
and trawled the airless nightmares of the drowned.

The shop still serves, with the front parlour added,
as off-licence. Teetotal George can't turn
in narrow plot. He won't root out his son,
wife, daughter-in-law on top or mum and dad

tucked in below. 'Not a dead cert, not quite,
miladdo. Suppose the dark is just the trick
light plays, tickled like me that look-a-like
shines his flashlamp down this shut, flooded pit.'

The Strap

Leather strap on the back door nail.
He'd belt us if we were naughty,
but never. We didn't know.
Never was future, moon-landings, our own cars.
Strap - shiny till you got close, saw
the cracks and scabby bits. His chin was like that
before he shaved. Hot water from the geyser,
the brush and shaving stick. And he kept on
looking and stroking. I do that with my beard.
Good lads most the time, our mum said.

Wouldn't have let him use it anyway.
But never. I sometimes think
just once he'd have enjoyed it, realised
he could do something. Not just work,
snooker, Woodbines, the pictures.
Thought I saw him once with another woman
five rows in front, got up, went home, forgot.
Did he? Did I dream?
Did the thought of her bare arm cross his mind
when the second ulcer burst?
By then mum and dad had moved and we
had wives and kids and lived away. The strap
went in the bin.
I wish they had had more excitement.
My kids look at me.
I wonder what they'll wish they'd wished for me
when it's quite safe, doesn't matter anyway.

Martha

We knew the cracks of every paving stone
down the back yard. Familiars in slow motion,
they told us nothing new, repeated jokes
every time we linked arm up in arm
and made procession to the outside lav,
silent as picture heroes flickering
through every weather the Lord God could chuck
at your rheumatics. How He'd tweak your bones,
climatic osteopath, to Whom you'd sing
Charles Wesley's anthems gritted through false teeth.
I almost had to lift you up the steps,
so you could shuffle round the door in boots
of black, that took ten minutes' bending down
to lace, and later that was my job too.

You wore them every day that you were up
and sitting on your chair-commode, a doll
dressed in long frock, clean pinnie, with your hair
in two tight plaits, braided across your head.
Eighteen and a prop forward, I could have
picked your skinny weight straight up and galloped
over the line, touched down between the posts,
but pain had got possession in the ruck.

Our kitchen stewed all those long summer days
with you, your bed, the pot-containing chair,
the sick-sweet smell that Dettol could not hide.
Teeth grinning underwater on the sill,
for eight slow weeks you did not take a bite,
but just drank milky tea and drooled and drooled,
hour upon hour, a long, unbroken skein
into the bucket nested on your lap
beneath the lump that grew, its thick grey fluid.

Talk had got stuck, you had to grunt and point
to tell us you had done for now. Buckets
had to be emptied too, and gradually
we were flushing you away, and always
your face was as pink and plain as a child's,
your eyes blue, your hands still, and so quiet
the lamentation only now arrives
after forty years' journey, grips as cold
as winters over Saddleworth's black hill.

You heard the news of my state scholarship
and gave a tiny smile, nod, touch of hand,
then slept again, your white unplaited hair
on the white pillow, while we ate our tea.
I half-heard movement in the night, but slept
weary with digging, mowing, marking-out
in parks and cemeteries and playing fields.
Dad woke us early, told us you had died
peaceful. Already you were gone, they'd thought
it best. But when you were brought back, they let
us look a minute into the coffin
where you lay all made up, your old straight face
painted the way you never could abide.

Young Clive said, 'That's not Grandma.' This set Mum,
who never cried much, crying. When we'd stripped
your bed, we carried it upstairs, a swap
for my old lumpy one. And the commode
went uphill too, in case, you never knew.
The kitchen stretched out like a new-lined pitch.

The Woods

My mother's siblings - not a word she'd use –
lived in still terraces of monochrome
with shadowy back-yards, front-gardens
where they grew tea-cups, sponge-cakes, trifles,
red salmon sandwiches and never moved
more than a street or two, unless they married
into a different album on the shelf,
dusty with coal and thick with cotton fluff.

They went to work and war, back to their house,
visited family and had family visit,
the kitchen full of women washing up,
the kitchen table giving kids house room,
while men played boredom with the clock that sat
on every mantelpiece and tocked and ticked
existence off while none of them were looking.
Before that, they'd creaked each night up wooden hills
and must have moved there sometimes to ward off
the upstairs chill and damp, to lift the weight
of eiderdown and blankets, must have moved
as I have cousins who are living proof,
a nurse, a printer, estate agent's clerk,
amateur twitcher, and a mayor of Rochdale.

All of us keep dead parents somewhere safe -
an attic or a cellar we don't use,
a cupboard under stairs, a cardboard suitcase -
where they can sit and goggle at the box,
wear Whitsun best, share a nice pot of tea
and never have to stir to see to us
or put coal on the fire. I visit them,
and all look ready for a good night's rest.

In her print pinnie, size of a scout tent,
Lizzie who lives up to her rhyme and keeps
both church and vicarage clean, makes Allen smile,
serious Allen, Leather wed to Wood.
Marie has flowery blouses and loud hats
and seems to keep her Ken moth-balled and pressed,
on a coat-hanger, ready when required.
Albert the gas man wears his uniform,
he has kind eyes that swirl in the thick swim
of marbled lenses that he glimpsed us through.
Harry wed Alice, lives next to the cut,
their street is shadowed by the spinning mill.
Herbert died 1900, nine months old,
and Margaret, leaving one girl, three boys,
at 39, when I was only two.

John (Jack), the youngest and the last to die,
lived happy in a heap of laughing kids
we gave up counting, he'd turned Catholic
for Edna, never regretted it, shows me
her photos, shy as if just engaged,
when he is eighty and has months to live
before their heavenly wedding date is fixed.
Nellie was first of ten and had to mother,
when mother died months after Jack was born,
the youngest kids. She stays kind to the end.
At Blackpool once with us her veins required
a rest, her and mum sharing an ornate seat
along the prom with some young couple.
She thanked them for the treat as we walked on.

And there is Joe, his arm, the wooden one
he got as stand-by for the one he'd left
in France. Too young to fight, he lied and went.
The doctor said he broke his mother's heart,
this soldier boy sent home, no further use.
He does not use the arm, it stays behind
a curtain by the door. I never asked,
will not get round to asking cousins now
who've spread themselves and little images
out over England, scattered like the sand
from Southport in a wild southwesterly,
the arm's last resting place. Did it burn in fire
or does it rot in earth like all the Woods,
Nancy, her siblings? Not a word she'd use.

The Superintendent

Freddie Bramwell: that to your face not one
of us would ever have dared call you
or even thought to breathe out such a note
of disrespect into the smoke-tattoo

that tanned your well-creased hide, Rev. F.T.B.
Cloth of your calling, given better weather,
would have sprouted baccy's huge greens
from its dark soils. But this was Lancashire,

coal, cotton, cables and the big, cold manse
triple-mounted with its red-brick, soot-stained
wall, black railings, gloomy laurels stiff
as my grandma's rheumatics when it rained.

Grammar school boy who, like you, read books,
you gave me time like there was no life after,
paid visits to our Martha and then talked
over her and teacups about literature.

You said nothing would please you more than me
being a minister, preaching the word
like you. But just one thing, if that call came
I should run off, defy it, wrestle hard,

wriggle out. Only if, pinned to God's earth,
I'd no escape, should I accept relief
from doubt. It was the worst job in the world
when turned to dust, despair and disbelief.

So now I wonder how you'd reconciled
your passions with the collar, only guess
the secret lay in those long Sunday sermons.
Performance artist of the word made flesh,

I loved your show, hung on your argument
from dark to bright, firebranding rhetoric,
tried pulpits on myself for fit, despite
your excellent advice to beat it quick.

You talked me into Iris Murdoch
just then come out in Penguin, half a crown,
and brought the stationer's to a dumbstruck stop
by ordering *Lady Chatterley*, first in town.

Your morning studies, sacred and profane,
stoked up your faith with strong St. Bruno's aid,
while Wesleyans in want of pentecosts
warmed to the tongue that licked across their heads.

I left to study English, you retired to read.

Conspiratorial

That morning, bare light will shake me,
crack each eye open like an egg,
start with its jumpy wires
my raw feet twitching, singe
my temples, dangle and dance me.

That morning, I will not know your name,
I will know nothing about you,
not your face, your identifying marks,
not the scar above your groin,
not one syllable I will tell, the truth.

That morning, the cosh of ignorance,
the sharp stick of denial
will pulp your bed to innocence,
a white-out, an absolution
on the ward's safe confessional.

That morning, you can tell me
where you will hide the body.
It is what I have. The loss like all loss
is required. *Hold on!* or something
you hiss, a cobra, a bronco.

That morning, here are its contents:
an arm's jerked jump the prayer,
the lock of hair a holy fragment,
closeness of smell that passes understanding
and your eye an empty tomb.

That morning, late or early
I'll be off somewhere. When they find me,
I will drive five hours into your night
waiting for me, our holding on.
All that long morning. They will never catch you.

How are you now?

The pile of papers you could not make out
are left me, with address-book out of date
and birthdays of the dead you'd quite forgot,
all witness to your mortal moonlight flit
to join them at the posh end of the street.

A better class of car outside the door,
while gilt on marble says you're 84
and Social Services won't call anymore.
You always said they didn't come before!
You got your wish, though, not to be put in care.

The cupboard's bare, the furniture's all gone,
the empty house has its *For Sale* sign on,
long-buried phrases trip out of the brain
empty as coal-trucks, clanking like their train:
I'm fine, much better thanks, the same again.

I'm better left alone, that's true enough,
and you have left me, that's another truth.
I'm just so glad that, though you fought it, tough
as the long, hard life, the stroke carried you off
and did not leave you without use, like stuff

- so much of it, we cleared the lot out, Nancy -
that shifts from jumble sale to sale and never once
gets bought. Alive, you led that dance
of bargain cardies, handbags, tranklements,
boots, shoes, a dusty troupe that took your fancy.

The gramophone went slower, came to its last stop
as the spring slackened. Like a spinning top
you stumbled into words, you dribbled
to a halt, you jerked like legend's alcoholic lop
that drank the bar dry, naming *The Last Drop*

with its last leap. A few miles down the street
you'd done the runner, hopped it, flit by moonlight,
landed on loves you thought you had forgot,
left me to face that riddle folk repeat,
sandpaper rhymes which still can't grasp at it.

Souvenirs

Right at the back of the wardrobe
Time I had a clear out
Heaps of old programmes.

Lost games with dead players
Somebody got fed up of them
Gave them to a nine year old.

He is 35 and lives in New York
With no space for souvenirs
So they have shared our house.

Can't bag them with today's paper
I stack them in a sort of order
The Boro, United, England, The Rest.

When I'm certified immortal
The kids won't have room for all this
Shall we chuck these or do you want them?

We all have this ghost in the spare room
It can't remember who it played for
But its dream goals duster the shelves.

A Place To Write

Under windows of shovelled sky, cloud stones,
under ceilings levelled with sun, lifted with rain,
I sit between air and earth, I scribble down
through floor-boards cracked with silence,
worm through books of soil. I squeeze my words

in this abandoned seam: water, foul air, roof-fall
prise workings open, undermine the house.
His pit-prop name scratches my retina: John Wood,
my mother's father, hewer of that coal,
who came up every shift, died in the light.

He goes back down, weighed deeper now
in the ply of family, layers of generation,
by his child's eighty heavy years,
my mother, Nancy, pitman's daughter
who has died in the pitmen's hospital.

His pick's turned marble, it taps out in me,
on this thin paper, at the shivered membrane.
He chips the words of bone, such imaginings
in tunnels low, hot, deep, confined.
A man could only crawl and not turn.

At last I am listening, there is a line
formed, their desires bursting up and out
in the ancestral queue, the breath fractured,
the languages bubble hot like springs of mud,
at last someone is listening, who should write it down.

But they must wait their turn, the last come first.
My mother is not ready yet to speak to me
and turns me back from all of them gone dead.
She leaves me with the living, with the seasons,
this place to write, surfaces not shored up.

Winter Breaks

1. Leaving

It's not my choice to go now,
this journey's lonely walk

Sheee's leaving home and each of us
understood, at every replay,
how reasonable all that was,
that she really couldn't stay.

Nor could many others her age
and older, though a lot of them
did stay put in the end, too small
for the magic boots, oh damn!

And our children have to do it,
estranged in the rites of success,
it's by now an expected feat
and we're their accomplices.

Snow, the long night, a winter moon,
the footstep clichés of Lonely
out onto the earth on her own,
come to flicker insanely

on the screen of each living room.
So many pilgrims of despair
paying the price of our freedom,
just see what they are in for.

Their wave's irresistible, sweeps
through every misery and pain;
the pull of the hunger of hope
overcomes all preventions.

And you, not wanting a fuss made
about anything trivial
as yourself, what will you decide
on leaving, arrival,

on the staying or returning?
Is it your dreaming or music
only, when all else is burning,
finds you a path through the dark?

2. Severe

Why should they mind my cuts and bruises?
Their child is now a wealthy bride.

An insane howl somewhere behind the gas fire,
autumnal from the south west, gives me notice,
the topsy-turvied earth launches its offensive,
minded to wipe me clean from its once smiling surface.

What happens as you get older is not just
balding head, hairy ears, the thickened toe-nails
you learn to lie with, but disenchantment severing
dreams, intentions in slices, feeding them to the gale.

Nobody gives a piss, registers a thing
some nursing home can't cure; they get wed, insured,
childed, no point telling the flattened aftermath.
In silence this sightless stuff must be heard out, endured.

3. Hopeless Case

If, my leaf, it falls to earth then,
nothing will my poor hopes save

The arboretum, mid-October, still
some leaves are holding on like the grim death
I don't want to imagine, but it comes
to grip some poor sod just as I draw breath.

And drinking coffee after in the shop
with scented soaps and books on trees and country
I join young Brokenheart of Schubert's *Reise*
watching one specimen fail to learn to fly.

All round us supine thousands on the grass,
you could not doubt the outcome of the bet,
for Brokenheart has seen enough leaves fall
to realise his losing streak and yet,

though I could pull out centuries of quotes
to show they're hackneyed, these German *mots tristes,*
and don't intend to snuff out young lost hopes
or play poetic death wish games, some beast

is out there, I have seen its marks, faces
of trampled mud, and I've become afraid
of tea shop troupers ordering flesh and blood,
this winter's menu faxed like a word from God.

4. Likeness

....a house that's warm and bright
and one dear soul that in it lies –
delusion is my only prize!

Like moth out of a flame,
like ice that's set on fire,
like discord in a choir,
like wanderer gone home.

Like cattle on a pyre,
like bee that keeps its bed,
like talking to the dead,
like honesty for hire.

Like fool wins three-card trick,
like acrobat off wire,
like love is like desire,
like cunt that turns to prick.

Like warming that's not drier,
like cold can burn like hot,
like it or like it not,
like told the truth, the liar.

5. Funereal

The dark will match my state of mind.

Might piss off now, get really pissed,
it's how much good I'm doing here
stuck out like a stale sponge finger
on plates piled off a wedding list.

What next? Nobody said, all plans
had been shovelled under the beds.
Someone, just warming to the touch,
left early to reach oblivion

before dawn fell. The tea's cold, rows
of sandwiches lie pale on slabs
of window-sills, the evening rays
beam condolence from some son-in-law

while the insane patter of wallpaper
dribs down like desiccated flies,
like me, obsessed with Orpheus,
most useless of undertakers.

But wasn't he a genius
with a line to the immortals
and music to charm their spears down?
If he were a god, he'd deliver us

from endings no-one here believes,
the hearsey-verse of dreamless sleep.
Anything but, a headless cluck,
limbs plucked to hell by girls in gloves.

And does it matter who she was
that has been so securely delivered?
The rules are strictly no returns,
no retrospective get-out clause.

It bloody matters if it's you, you
still pretending that it doesn't, all tight-eyed.
I'd want to bang mine out on railings
just to show you, just to show.

6. Restoration

with feet that drag me down,
through life that's bright and happy

A sky stuffed with light, the North Sea flattened
under off-shore wind, gusts steer me and suck sideways,
concessionary tripper to this war zone,
sheep grazing the cavities, all that is carious.

For us there is nothing to do out here but rot,
the bony curtain wall, the slackening teeth.
Bright plastic bottles keep their colour up,
carry it off every storm, top the fringe of wrack.

Across old landfalls jets scud low, invade
our failing hearing, lock on crumbling towers.
Flower-lists in churches allocate a future,
gulls hang on up there, shriek to the last herring.

Time drags more-often-stumbling legs along
the shifty edge of wet and dry, I tell myself,
don't be so bloody miserable, a great day out
ends well with crab and pint in the hostelry.

It's *The Jolly Fisherman*, so all aboard.
The dead raise glasses to the waiting ocean,
drink to their winter breaks, fish bones up from the soup.
Boat people drown out there to join these classes.

7. Warming

*as if you'd melt the total
of all the winter's ice*

Deep winter? Not more than icing on rich cake of winters,
on tree-trunk, on onion, on gobstopper, on stick of rock
we are saying suck to, so many ice cubes left to dreg away
in glasses' tepid guts in a pub with gas-log fires.

The last place I saw you. A tear tightroping each lower eyelid
under a live game all fouls, falls, penalties, red cards
as if it was fair or expected that you should carry such a world
on your head like a chill jug of water, had to haul from a deep well.

The ref's a shite! As well anthems spout from the sheer faces,
the clamorous, watching dead. You always turned the sound down,
will find it hard to believe I'm drowning, swept off, molten,
and it was something you'd let slip, set the heart on defrost, said.

8. Disposal

Come on, my friend, you'll find here
a resting place, you'll see.

It's earth or sky, unless you're lost at sea.
I'd much prefer the earth, though not straight rows
where far too many lie gift-trussed, God knows,
like last year's turkeys nobody will buy.

There's churchyards (moss, sheep, arty lichen).
These might get booked up lifetimes in advance,
but vicars could have cards and sermon stamps
so you could earn safekeeping near an icon.

I've heard, like most things now, you can go green,
although I'd always noted dead meat did.
You plant a tree, save offspring several quid
with cardboard box, a folksong or a keen.

Frustrating though, that you can't pass right through it,
the burgeoning wood trunk that's part and parcel,
to take the whisper out of passing arseholes
and terrify their daylights with a fart.

Curmudgeon living as curmudgeon dead,
recycling eternities of grumps
till tree dies also, becomes bonfire chumps,
and that's the bottom to it, I'm cremated.

So bugger me, leave me to worms and flies,
not worth consideration by grim reaper.
Good pickings to be had elsewhere and cheaper
where harvest home is falling from the skies.

9. Recall

How differently you made me welcome,
you fickle and inconstant town!
Lark, nightingale, each lit your windows
and strove to sing the other down.

Remembering the exact spot where
this happened or, if not this, that,
is harder than it appeared in first light
stamping approval on desired, then handheld beauty
as I did yours and do recall the light or rather
the flesh on which it fell or into which its fill
cascaded, but not the number or the street at all.
To say this is not to say it was done casually.

Returning now would be to pull down, tear
the fabric of the old and rotten curtain
I've patched up against birdsong and the dawn,
their treacherous disposition to be sunny
as my first falling in was, seems still so
where it has gone. An old mind plays tricks, games
and with itself, no choice, those sodden dreams
through which breath creaks, pulse coughs, heart staggers flimsy.

10. Notice

And when the cocks crowed early,
my heart was wakened wide

Off for the winter, are you? Bloody hell!
And with old you-know-who along as well?
No need to add explanatory text,
just leave me wondering what you'll tell me next!

Not that I've ever fancied winter sports,
the snazzy awful clothes, the grim reports
of avalanches, all that après-ski,
this is the stuff brings out the worst in me,

the opposite of all the things you like.
When fear kicks in, the nice parts go on strike,
you told me what they were once, can't recall,
but winter sports craps white-out on them all.

You look as if to say you'd thought I might
go thick-eyed as a damp November night
and typically forget to think that spring
will come and you with it, appearing

like what's-her-name from out the underworld,
your face all sun-tanned and your legs unfurled.
I don't forget. If looks could resurrect,
I'd melt the sodden lot, leave winter wrecked,

have all its sports slopped soggy down the drain,
so I could live full-time with you again
in light and warm and dry, not give a shit
what happened to the global warming bit.

You could snap back there never was a time
when we had that arrangement, but your rhyme
to my disgruntlement's infantile myth
is softer, subtler, telling me the truth

and that it's seasonal, its ebbs and flows,
synapses, snaps, stanzaic body-blows
are hymns to love, antiphonal, at odds
with what we dream of snatching from the gods.

As usual, you'll persuade me that's the way,
I'll start the countdown day by bloody day,
hoping next spring and summer lie ahead,
knowing each one is one less till we're dead.

11. Zero

My heart is like a dead thing,
her cold stare deep inside.

Look at it like I showed you,
like a photograph, you have to
keep on choosing what to put
in your little dancing handbag
stapled to a snow wall
anything could penetrate anytime just
there. Smart, that third dimension,
splits kisses, rips nails.

You stiffened like ice cream
to my freezer fingers
in your cardboard pyjamas,
there was a hint of melting,
of berry juice slices,
a taste at the far end of the signal's range,
maybe a 747 going down unauthorised,
breath knotted in bellies.

Trees smashing light back,
salt sprinkled on leaves, rubble
of angels, the water building
itself down, a white wax candle
that can fuck granite
and does. Hold me responsible,
that edge of rock, that drop in the eyeball,
scratches in a cold blue.

12. Circular

The post brings none to you addressed

That morning was so dark, it made me shift
to raise the blind, it was the sky. So far
so good, and then they dropped with dead flies' drift
through the door's slot, first shots of festive fare
from friends who scratch my grudges every year.

Don't need to open them, watch it go by
the weather out there, listen to the clock
cough, you know their parents died or will die
soon enough, or they've split up, but will attack
once more their wed address list, sound heroic.

My age and literate, what's to be done?
Let them write out last year's disaster list
and demonstrate how we must cope and grin
when genius kids are middle-aging fast,
poor specimens of what the future's passed.

They're managing, not companies or gangs,
but getting by, and they are keeping jolly
as muscle shrinks, as joints give out, most things
work with a something aid, and gradually
plastic and steel replace the flesh's folly.

Their celebration is that they survive
and I'm supposed to raise my glass to that,
treasure their trips in photographic trove,
sundown safari or the cruise round Crete.
You have to see the sunny side of fate,

I guess, to be a golfer, bash your balls
across some crimplene cow-cleared meadowland,
or go to adult ed., sit in cold halls,
empty your flask while cluttering your mind
with stuff the temporary staff don't understand.

If, it's not likely, any of them read this
and take offence at my ingratitude,
they might feel I am extracting the piss,
finding their kind intentions misconstrued.
My lifelong learning is in being rude.

Putting it blunt, a card will do next time,
merry old mash, happy new mish, such shlock,
which is all that I need to hear from them
on the other side. It's a piece of cake,
a candle, somebody there when I knock.

13. Freeze

Snow, you know all my desires:
Now where do you want to go?

Think of yourself as a glacier by all means, the progeny
of deep winter, will give a reassurance in the coldness,
the solidity, the hands-off-me slippiness of surface.
You will not though be able to deny that there is movement

and that it is towards me, inevitable, the ice's pull
downhill, out from the cold core, to where it finds some warmth,
and that this movement at its adventurous extremity
melts to a flow that is simply water and feeds springtime.

Not so simple. If the earth is cracked in the head, infected
or insane, poisoned, made war on, if it's in raging fever,
what can save you from liquidity, from the defencelessness,
the wetness of love? Or rescue me from the weight of such tears?

Trying too hard. Only a lump of flesh that's past its freshest,
that grows chill across the shoulders, at the softness of the back,
as in a damp night late in my years I write and cannot know
what gets by through thin air to where you may not feel the cold

or where you sit inside the mind of a new house, whether you
are making order of so much snow, packing it into chests,
loading the shelves with it, reading its not-to-be-deciphered sounds
or playing them on refrigerators, the silent white keys.

14. Stuff

Into your hide I'm etching
with one well-pointed stone

There's so much singing about Brokenheart,
I sometimes think nobody reads the script,
a general lack of will to prise apart
the lips of pity-me in which he's zipped.

And all those images he screws from winter,
the ice, the snow, the dark, the crows, the storms,
has any psychoanalyst looked into
his wanton deviation from the norms?

A layman's view, of course it is, but I think
poor Brokenheart had never had a fuck,
his fantasies as frigid as the ice rink
round which he never skated, no such luck,

had to make hay with frozen river bed,
which seems a paradigm of virgin lust,
a frosty mirror of the most frustrated
scratching away at its inviolate crust.

Smooth talker that her parents sent back packing?
Or were his moor-top tantrums justified?
Perhaps he stalked her? Was he always slacking
or, as he claimed, gazumped over this bride?

My own view is, as stated, he'd not had her
and slung his hook before she called his bluff.
That makes this wintry stuff seem even sadder
to one who never feels he's had enough.

You don't reply, you're silent on the topic,
you like the music, never mind the text.
Perhaps you'd like me to be philosophic
at my age and not talk so over-sexed.

Still not a word, and shit you might be thinking:
How long since that I saw him with a hard-on,
if only he could slow up with the drinking,
I'll put a CD on, plan next spring's garden.

And sure enough you shove one in the slot,
adjust the volume till the ceiling knocks,
it's poor pale Schubert *über* all the lot
a year before he died of Spanish pox.

15. Collection

Joy and sadness, all our caring,
are this light's misleading game.

The light's eternal, so I'm done, that's it,
locked into holy day, its collection box,
a roof of angels that mum lullabies.

Up through the slot, against the drip of pence,
I shove this out on an old biro, it's
my last communiqué on my last ten quid.

So, if you want, see the light, be born again,
just forget anything I felt or said
for you, to you, and get rid of the tapes.

All the moaning and groaning we did,
blew it on the wrong horse, liked its name and
no more waste of time than all the rest.

You could get your revenge, you could curse
some god for my metamorphosis, small change,
join in the hymns or pull the temple down.

But I'd rather you left me quick and ran
back into the dark, love, of primroses,
might be a few left, before the bright sky drops.

16. Accommodation

Are all the rooms in this house
already occupied?

Another wintry visit to the Crem,
increasingly those late night phone calls come
with their reminders: life is but a dream,
morning no more than *in memoriam*.

It's rather like the Post House down the road,
same bricks, same shrubs and lawns, same chimney stack.
I wonder if they offer bed and board,
ask at the desk, but no-one answers back.

Now I am envying (you as well?) the sod
who's made it to the safety of the casket
and wishing it was me up there instead,
the Roller, silk sheets, chicken in the basket.

No Vacancies and not *Abide with me*
the tape's repeating on the life machine.
Don't hang about, piss off and get your tea,
you're at death's door though, keep your knickers clean.

17. Liberty : A Letter

I'm set to finish with all this seeming –
why stay around with all these who're dreaming?

When it rains, filth concentrates.
All that floats, swirls to the lake
we filter for our water. Little to do.
The mounds of waste collapse and spread,
beer cans, baked bean tins. Plastic bags
heave to be free of barbed wire fencing.

And with the rains the grass grows
thick and tall, the waste gets hurled
from cars, it is not collected.
I worked for this, fought for it,
I am in a bad mood, yes.
Election rally, speakers blaring,
then the outdoors party,
all night, the hi-fi was a taxi,
ugh you are mine tonight ugh ugh.
I get the music free, throw the empties,
the discarded knickers, back
into the neighbours' drive.
Better stop, this is not poetry.

I see the pains love brings to
mismatched lovers, how they
cling to it, worship the thing,
love. My game is played. Copped out,
said that I could not love her,
lied to myself, knew all things
were possible, that one step
into the dark, if taken.
I have enough to handle.
All kinds of things there are
to keep me awake at night,
and all preferred to poking
of Eros or Venus yielding.

Not supposed to be writing
about myself, forgive an old man.
The last to ask what I think
of your poems, can tell you though,
like music, the colours they are.

18. Soap

my one road is all demanding,
this way nobody comes back.

This Brokenheart cannot resist a symbol,
packs his brain-fevered haystacks in a thimble,
this way his psychological distress
has come by now to sound like nothing less

than human sense of universal loss;
life, beauty, love, youth, well we all get cross
with such bereavements, such departures:
just watch *Eastenders*, listen to *The Archers*.

A common lot, it's crap, but Brokenheart
thinks his is special, worth more than a fart,
so traffic lights that stop him are mock suns
and road signs give the foolish boy the runs.

The car he's twocced careers out of control,
the road's as finite as a toilet roll,
the final perforation comes, and shit!
But there's much more than metaphor to it,

much more than young idealist martyrs think.
Rushing to push the world over the brink,
they tear themselves to shreddies, shred, shred, shred.
Makes little difference when they're good and dead.

Old sods like me, useful as rotten rope,
we still hang on in there, without much hope,
for one last exit from the one-way street,
an unmarked by-road, secret way to cheat

Old Sod Himself with one more episode
of *Freude ohne Schaden*, get our load
of booze, of sex, whatever's branded sinful,
shake it all over till we've had a skinful.

While Brokenheart's at his symbolic signing,
where every silver cloud has a black lining,
he could be winning millions of fans
snogging on sofas, pilfering from vans,

become the winner of the next *Big Brother* -
life mimics art, one bad show breeds another,
or star in *Crossroads*, one sure way to send
dead-ended dick round his last peaceful bend.

19. Waiting

so that I hate my youth's long day –
the grave's rest still so far!

Late January, under the church wall's height
the snowdrops struggle out, their papery white
as sparse and pale as hairs left in my head.
Their anchors are the chalked lines of the dead.

The year that's gone, so far from what we guessed,
the worst much worse, the good far from the best,
the new graves not those that we had predicted,
our choice of plot by these that much restricted.

Now, as the footpaths open up and stick
swings round and thwacks to raise the bramble's sneck,
the gales sweep in and turn the fields to flood,
the resurrected sheep are fleeced in mud.

These summaries of day in winter's long
and whining *tenebrae*, that lights-out song,
these snowdrops rise, their paper white as bone,
brief IOUs, on which I could write down

the debts I owe you, love, this time of year
when hope and joy get trampled under fear,
attraction shrinks all shrivelled in the cold
and passion hugs its blanket damp with mould.

The dead beat grasses lying in my way
will lift their seed-heads to the longest day,
so everything will come to one who waits
with fading snowdrops by the churchyard gates.

20. Rambler

My heart sees in the heavens
its picture painted bold –
it's nothing else but winter,
a winter wild and cold!

Go walking where you'll meet no bugger else,
get up them hills, let winds of winter bray
each inch of skin, of flesh, of skeleton
and whittle eyes down onto *imago*.

Project your heart's bleeding content out
on that blockbuster sky, don't give a sod -
burnt bracken's casting couch lacks an incumbent,
like bed back home it's damp, cold, empty, hard.

Spoil-heaps and their old mines are such refusals
as grow you lumps, subside you, shaft your throat;
plantation conifers stride down the fellside,
skin-prickling dreams, you shiver, want to shit.

The sun has turned its arse, pale as a camp child,
on death's rollover total, flaunts its moons
brightblinding fence-posts, can't help but remind
you're the remainder of these long divisions:

last human on the shelf of winter's planet,
one writer-reader, *poeta ergo sum*.
Convivial as wanking, hopeful as a sperm bank,
when you feel bad, up here's the place you'll come.

21. Call

Crow, why won't you, strangest bird,
leave me isolated?

Yes, I am on the train.
What's that? The terrible din?
It's the crows, they crowded in,
packed every other seat.

Raucous and getting louder
with every can they spike – yes, lager,
I've tried the crossword in the paper
but I can't concentrate.

At every sodding station
a detachment stands to attention,
pecks its way in, pushing
what's left of air and light.

And now they insist that I sing
and this to their accompanying
undertow, the mass of beating wings,
the tables' thump: *'Exterminate!'*

Soon we will arrive, on time,
each crow in the dark gone home
well dined, leaving only bone
for which crows are too delicate.

Lost property, white knuckled grip,
bird of my hand, its brittle clip
still holding in its bite the heap
of poems, love, you'll get too late.

22. Resolve

Then ourselves we'll be gods!

Frost shut down eyes,
snow whitewash beard,
ice thicken blood,
hail stone all tears.

Let the tears not melt
for joy or pain,
let the frozen crud
sit tight in the vein.

Indifferent as god
on a distant throne,
impassive and hard
as the heart never felt.

23. Love Song

before this, walking kept me cheered,
the barren tracks my testing

When you keep going you keep going.
I'm telling you. I'm telling you
you keep going you stay warm.
When you're managing you keep moving.

When you change it you stay alive
you're moving you're staying warm.
You remind me I forget that
you are managing, keeping going.

When you mind it you stay warm.
I'm telling you, I'm telling you
when you keep going you keep going,
staying alive, keep it moving.

I remind you. You forget that
if you're moving you're staying warm.
When you manage it you keep moving,
staying alive and keep it changing.

When you're managing you keep warm.
I'm telling you, I'm telling you.
You stay alive, you keep going,
you're moving, it's forgetting.

You stop changing, you get moved.
You're reminding to keep forgetting.
You stop moving, you get cold.
I'm telling you, you stay going.

I forget who. You remind me
when you're going you keep moving.
Stop the changing, staying tired of,
getting minded, can't be managing.

You stop living, you stay dead.
Are you minding, are you telling me
you forget how? I'm getting to.
Can't be changing what's reminding.

You're done to, you're changed past,
you're moved by, you're cold down,
I mind when, alive who,
staying gone, I am telling you.

24. Stranger

Shall I, strange old fellow,
with you go along?
Will you turn your organ
grinding to my song?

I sent my poem walking,
limps by on these lame feet.
You might observe it stalking
along your music's street.

It's written on the pension,
born of an old man's pain;
if it caught your attention,
wouldn't have lived in vain.

You took life's short-lived verses
and made their lyrics sing.
If old curmudgeon's curses
could start such wandering,

so he might learn delight of
your wintry harmonies,
might even get a sight of
love and such mysteries.

Young man, go on your travels
and never once look back
at sorrow that unravels,
at promises gone slack.

Verlangen deine Lieder
nach Liebe, stirbt sie nicht.
Orpheus kommt nicht wieder,
hinkt vorbei mein Gedicht.

Love lives on in the yearning
of songs and will not die.
Orpheus not returning,
my poem hobbles by.

Inventing the Tenses

We have taken to it like ducks to champagne,
inventing the mythic tenses with a duck-billed smile,
paddling and breasting swirls of our rivery story.

Not one of us remembers that past indefinite,
its ripped fish, its muddy bottoms. Glass-eyed,
we let all that drop into the drink.

Our forward waddle's to the future imperfect,
its well-quacked failings, its cork-tight excuses,
champagne swooshing off ducks' backs.

No point pecking over the pluperfect indicative
gone and done with before ducks were involved.
So bottoms up, not worth drowning over.

Over the present inedible we argue endlessly,
stabbing and chewing its white slices,
the plastic packaging, knowing it is bad for us.

We could get used to this, subordinate imperative,
like ducks to the laughter
sinking each other and without tears.

Viewer

News item: In the States there are now more pornographic
video shops than there are Macdonalds restaurants.

My father was a stud in hardcore film,
His crotch full as a sail, well hung
Between strong masts. He took the helm,
Could pilot weaker vessels with his tongue.

An expert. He applied his country craft,
Fixing each piece of earth with his ploughshare
That furrowed deep. Dust, breaking on his shaft,
Lifted its treasure to the sky's bright stare.

Reined mares, the sweating flanks rolled round
And back into the soil. His eye
Narrowed, long lens angled. In he ground,
Coming on cue, in line, exactly.

I wanted to grow up and plough,
To close one eye, stiffen my sex.
But all I did was watch him. How
His pale flesh banged on who came next.

I tripped and fell upon his stallion's work.
His dying whinnies filled that autumn day.
He left me only all this thrust and jerk,
The harnessed, harrowed ghosts I play and play.

Reading Your Spine

as night and daylight turn
fonts of skin, faded erasures,
bones' braille, each coiled crux.

I excavate the down of script,
I can't disturb your sleep
with my soft scrape of verse.

You'd closed the book, you'd slipped
through the unlettered door,
you'd gone down silent

to the obscure depths
I can't reach, can't make out,
all that's authorial.

Text you would proof in the glass,
illustrate as you dressed,
teach me by heart,

it's at my fingertips.
If you were to open again
on the tender stalks of my eyes.

Tomb Decoration: Cattle

Not a breath. It was the painter's rod
froze these waves hard,
assault-craft beefing up the last resort,
a troupe lifting repeated legs all down the line,
skimming a cresty froth from the pigments' tide.
Their cloned accompaniment beyond decay
mimes *Moo-mummify-me*,
they promenade the years to here.

Goggle at the symmetry of this chorus,
admire the delicate boy, his arm
signing them forward, young god of the surf.
He carries rope in a coil, the star of the show,
the hangman, the saviour who can light the fuse,
set the spangled heap to bonfire.

We can't expect them just to swagger on,
hot rasps from nose and throat,
the hitch up of a tail, a flood
of steamy piss or runny shit,
the hustling of flies around an ear,
the glitter that stirks' eyes are brainy with.

But here they come again
stitching their final sequence in reverse,
shuffling it subtly so it's hardly noticed.
They'll not miss a good funeral,
hoofing it two soft shoes at a time
up the steep dive of the escalator.

All that rehearsal for
the silent months of quarantine.
Their eyes fill with the indifference
cows practise when their calves are taken
and they swell with milk, make statues
in the dusky grass at long past milking.

Song for Mario

More than an island
you were learning to sail
on those choppy words
a little boat to
maybe, one day, Chile.

And into your being,
lover, communist, martyr, poet.
You found your silence, you sang it
under boots, under truncheons.
The redness inside you, outside you.

The damage of poems
that change the impossible.
Is the whole world a metaphor?
you asked that poet.
A circle on a blank page.

There it goes, small white ball,
riots through all the defence.
Your woman's mouth secretes it,
your son's hand holds it.
Little white ball of earth
shoots the circumference.

And there you go,
almost silent fish,
escaping the sad nets
with the tide's blood.
Maybe, one day, Chile.

This Once

It might have been a ready sack of daughter,
gift-wrapped, weighed in, in waiting for
just one unchosen suitor's trick,
his sleight, his slicky sense of balance,
his right deposit on the scales: could be
a crafty answer, virtual estates, a clever dick;
or three little piggy banks stuffed with stolen gold
till their bellies crack, their glass eyes pop;
or the head of an ogre, speechless at this atrocity.
Might have, might not have been.

There is a legend of a father taken off
such distances before his daughter's birth,
she searched the ball of earth seven times,
she set aside a sacred ground,
cut from her soul, to make his grave
when she could find him.
Almost at last she did,
buried and somewhere else and quite content.
Her soul might possibly be mended if
there is or isn't such a legend.

Suppose it was three or four dips
into the springs of the connubial,
the steamy lake with the lifting sword,
the warmed-up chlorines, the whirlpool spa,
all that mixed bathing, those bacteria,
the how to paddle, the how to tread
the up-to-your-chin-full, the how to pull
a bronze award for dripping, gasping causes,
the how far down the deep end leads.
Suppose it wasn't.

Imagine there is someone not deceived
by what tom talking-cat drops on the step,
who never buys his purring prospect
or orders him those fur boots from the catalogue,
or the hat with a feather, not one special offer,
not one tit for all his rat-a-tat.
But lets him in the door
to share the fire and toast his claws,
hums the tune along to his repeated plaintive promises.
You can't imagine?

Believe it, at the bottom of the garden
this muddy-laboured dryad,
her fertile nails fingering out from dirt
its tough, implausible offspring.
Her clay-bound feet, her skyward eyes,
dresses of leaf-mould, rainy song,
her stumping after trees,
her wishing to be done,
her hanging on, her pangs of birth.
Believe it or not.

That's the direction, as far as it's got,
the last stop, the white space, the page top.
Dangling those weary-wise tell-tale puppies
over the drop in a sack on a finger end.
It could be the place to start
bouncing incredulous bungee history
till it shivers in mid-air stasis,
tough and defenceless as the new-born,
seconds to spare before this
once this upon this a this time.

In the Purse

I lost it years ago and never guessed
it slipped straight down between the lining
and the leather, lay there flat and stiff
as kids in long grass, playing dead.

I tired of looking for it, thought it best
obliterated with one wipe. I watched
the dust put coats on sills, on lintels, breath
that counted to ten thousand while you hid.

Ready or not. Up cracked stairs. Our almost
empty room. One cupboard jammed with damp.
Inside it, swaddled in that moth-chewed fur
your mother wanted me to wear (I never did),

the purse I carried when we wed. I twist
the rusted clasp, let fingers in again,
follow them down into the frayed silk seams
and find it, sick of being sought, not glad

to have its boniness fished out at last,
a grey-faced relic from its shabby shrine,
lining and leather. Love, is that all it was,
your name on it, and all I ever had?

Sunday Morning, Reading Drabble

who mentions a gnarled hand
with its embedded ring.
At least I haven't yet
got my hands gnarled,
the ring is loose enough
just wedged below the joint.

Troubled, I still look down -
not quite gnarled, though gnarling
if clock's hands can gnarl.
Or is it 'being gnarled'
as trees that ring our years
fall in this October
all their leaves out there
where next door's building
a conservatory, the sun's new trap
on shared south-facing wall?

If we tried to spring that snap
on godhead, snaky-haired,
so feared and revelled in?
Divinity that sets us bait,
lets us build our cages, has us
write *if he is willing* in inky flame
on every policy we're sold.
It has given us fire,
watches us torch our own,
roast the whole street indeed.
It watches anything but.
Each tedious outrage filed under heaven,
a claim on deficit interest.

Sunday, early trees and silence.
The sun slips into winter,
light-fingers through the pages
its secularity, touches such questions
as are here in morning
where absent author plays
with gnarling reader, takes this day
of not-for-long autumnal brightness
at its best, does not quite find faith
in inconclusive loveliness,
the life short and almost unbearable.

Manhattan Piece

After midnight, a one-way,
rain hosing brake-lights
into the gutters, legless,
squealing, a blaze of eyes.

Inching between
parked metal-shine,
moving metal-shine.
WALK / DON'T WALK
he is doing both.

Has the ripped umbrella up,
a bag full of stuff,
coat without buttons,
rest too dark to see
but the cardboard square
at his chest wet through.

He walks / does not walk
into the darkness,
swirls of rain, electric red.
The numbered streets
lead all ways to deep water.
The city pumps in neon blood.

Has the face of a hero,
broken stone, grimed stone,
face like a lost star.
That flickering, patient sky.
Insect aircraft pinned up there
offering the sacraments.

The Afternoon Slot

Post-Impressionism, Middlesbrough
reads the label on the box, it is one
of six dun-cow-discoloured boxes stacked
beneath the radiator, draped with coats
we dropped with bags that spill their papers out.
The other boxes' labels too far off
to read in lecture room, this adult class
writing out solitary sentences.

Writing out solitary sentences
serves as a seventh box of sorts, it lacks
the alloy handles, rivets down each edge,
cupped corners, reinforcing strips.
The table shivers to pen-pushing time,
the tutor scatters carpet's bleary blue
with photographs of gravestones by the yard,
of mausolea and of cenotaphs.

Of mausolea and of cenotaphs,
a monochrome confetti-fall of ash,
we could soon get sick. Who's it for, this box?
What might be mouldering away in there?
A plant about to go critical with
an after-life we must prick out in verse,
so aching long to learn post-kingdom-come?
Endeavour and Discovery, lift the lid!

Endeavour and discovery lift the lid
expecting brushes, oils, intense sensation,
sharp palette knife, *la vie*, a roseate
pointilliste impressioning - but we find,
corrected, Teesside colour proofs, the prints
of post-industrial green fields, remains
of charnel towers that swallowed fire and sky:
Post-Impressionism, Middlesbrough.

Early June 2003, Grandchildren

Sunday afternoon. Not one snip of cloud.
The mouse in the kitchen skirting
recumbent for its final siesta.
Next door the TV talks in its sleep,
too fast, it gives the game away,
the Grand Prix racing, Eurosport,
the calculating whine, the cicadas
corporate and circling. Sky,
getting warm, so Spain, somewhere close
where life goes extending the airport,
the flyovers, the centre of nations.
Pulling tight the belt: *residencia,*
barrio commercial, condominio.
And any day now our second grandchild
on cue for crowd scenes, the cast of thousands
in the heavy wings of her waiting.

Two-year-old hand and voice signal 'plane'
up in a sort of heaven and we say 'yes',
do not pull him from the terrace
or force him three steps at a time
into the basement's chill.
We sit tight over dinner, look where
only the darkness falls
on the capital streets. Below us
the trains run clean and regular, white rats.
Perched in their orthodontic grins
the oldest *paisanos*, suckled when bombs
outnumbered rains and the fields
let burn, left uncut. They smile up
small and contentedly at their teenagers,
admire the scaffold-work of two generations.

So come and be about it, little one,
before the hottest of days hits town.
Who knows what we make of each other
or say when it's our lines to speak,
madrileña and you, her Manhattan brother?

Beethoven Back of Blencarn

jostles the dark, elbows the
dirty-windowed road
aside, pulls two rabbits
out of its hedges
and over its ears.

You rabbits, you two
fur-lined stiffies
in the full-beam frazzle
defrosting those lollopy legs
will you just
stagger it staccato it
hop it to the verge and
melt into the dark
spare me the dazzle?

I'm in a fierce noisy starship
I'm staring in the uncertain
I'm swooping the blinded road
I'm a-hunting a-kenning a-peeling-off
the pity and illumination.

Here's speaker-spitting applause
here's two rabbits
between road edges
between galaxies
here's my fingers hung
on the whirly wheel
my eyes shrinking and swelling
here's a torchlight of questions
here's a terror of bright
here's my ears slinking
in the skulk hole of a dead man
the skull hulk of a deaf man

who is jostling again
always elbowing
into the major
telling me to listen
as if he knows the way
beyond the throw of the light.

The Price You Pay

I was cycling to the rainbow,
the near end, one tree more luminous
than the rest, that copse six long fields off.

Every road was a trough, a wash, a this-is-
what-happens when the tears flow,
a tyre-to-mudguard swish of sorrows, sorrows.

And I was asking for that trouble, good grief,
cycling to the rainbow where it leapt
between the darks of cloud cliff and fellside.

Round Culgaith, a man on the back lane,
a man with five spaniels leashed out in a spray.
It's the price you pay for rainbows, I told him.

Now, after Skirwith, Ousby, fourteen miles,
all of it poured over, and me dry-skating through
puddles of shiny sky, the clean blue cheek of it.

Trees shaking wet green fleeces, they pelt their
hand-me-downpours at anyone passing,
still miss me, parched as a proper summer.

The last few yards, unmade, uphill, are not impressed
and ditch me sideways. The bike scrapes four cog-teeth
in bloody parallels above the hoof. To teach me.

But it won't. Not yet. A rainbow on two wheels,
of course which can't exist. While it does,
ride the impossible, breathable, proof.

At St. Leonard's

i.m. Roger Kirk, York, January 2003

Visiting you the last time
in the low slant of daylight
I met you lying at the sun's edge
where you could see the funny side
and haul yourself onto it
when your back got weary
of the serious business
with its indoors and ceilings.

So you did, you turned
to watch a solemn comedy,
me dropping your catch of words
unruly syllables we could not get in line.

Then taking me unawares
you stretched your hand to my face
fastened your fingers on my nose
wagged it so curiously
from side to side.

Perhaps it was a thing
you had wanted to do
years ago, one of those meetings
in your office, instead of coffee,
or over dinner, generous host,
to substitute a second glass.
But what you told me
smiling as you bent it
I lacked the language for
sensing some honour in this tender mischief.

And now you are still.
Spring in your garden
will grow full of your wisdom.
Birds will nest in its hedgerow,
bulbs burn with its energy.
It was always the young
you worked for, the future
you spoke to, the light
you understood as everlasting.

I should think of you in terms
of courage, of a kind gentleness
but that's not the way of it
when a good man's died.
You'd tweak me for abstraction.
I'll remember the first flower
of the year you had lived to see
brought by love from home.
There in a little glass, bright beside you.
Or sometimes in the mirror
I'll give my rubbery nose a twist or two,
recall your enigmatic punch-line
and wonder, when I catch you up,
if I'll have got the joke.

No Ice

for John Macleod

Glenlivet 12, cheers,
no water thanks, no ice.
There's just me in the bar,
I don't ask twice.
The barman knows my taste
and fills my glass
without a second glance
to make this long night pass.
The others left the warmth,
the light, my company
on some wild goose hunt
for divinity.

Some new-born baby
in the pub-yard shed,
I don't know yet
if it's alive or dead
or what on God's earth
it is doing there
with two dead tractors
and a cracked-up chair.

They soon come back,
they're shivering with cold,
then by the open fire
the tale gets told.
I hear the yearly nonsense
about stars and sheep,
voices from up the sky,
it makes a wise man weep.

They do still look amazed
and they are really nice
to everyone. Won't last,
I get my order in, precise:
Glenlivet 12, cheers,
no water thanks, no ice.

April in Coach B

Beneath the strains of divine and comic Joseph Haydn
fellow-passengers are whimpering far too loudly
their re-tread secrets, then raising their voices for each
unanimous and soulless verdict e.g. 'Dad'll go
mad.' Agreed, but, God, the waste of breath you've put
in train, trundling us nearer heaven's mouth or what
lies in the waiting room. It's April in coach B
and offspring jumping on the seats, leaping
like cuckoo clocks, moaning like collared doves
when mother-handled down while a woodpecker
hammers - was it here or there? - in mobile tones. Big Joe
looks up from his dancing needles, says to give it time,
and in his knotting swirls of air repeats the given time,
the gift of time, time handed over. It is true our
eyes are glazing, batteries fail, all texts decay.
Birch, oak, ash dream us for their counted sheep
as the quartet rolls *vivace* with a heave to a stop,
to a station, to a silent platform
where the song is change.

Hand

Left or right
just you now
finding and hitting keys
deciphering the codes
press, pin, unleash
dins past counting.

Do your legerdemain
your sort of stuff
the flicking and flexing
the levitation, the prestidigitation
the finger-painting, the sleight and
dance in the gravitational field
of this one star in black and white
this great growler of a star
song in its belly like a trapped wind
you stroking and slapping and tickling it
till it howls.

All that bone china
firing, spinning the air, whooping.

When the corruptible
is become incorruptible
when the song is wind through sand
when you are at the smallness of grain
your little bones, your lost teeth
your drifting scales, your white fish-stones
scattered in silent wholes on vacant staves
and love's sigh gone into the blue
where stars just hum, the real state of things
the sign of storms once in that fall of sand.

Hand, for the hot and cold
of what this heart is
count out its bars
beat on them while you can
with hammers at anvils
with strings, with furnaces, with tears
all hand on this tempestuous deck
to batter out the birth of it
melt and mould the gleam of it
to the breathing air.

Calvary

In this oak screen there's symmetry at least,
the windowed sun cross-membered by a Christ,
his face rubbed almost featureless.

Framework and trunk of this earth's map:
the head set north, feet nailed to south;
arms in their soft ellipses
stretch fingers east and west.

Each pane mirrors across. Above
two angels comfort or two devils taunt.
Both lean one elbow on the crucifix,
both stretch their tongue-curled wings,
both set a footprint on one chiselled wrist.

Two sharp-nosed pikemen, sure of their place beneath,
align their shafts, south-east, south-west,
inwith the grain of flesh. One constant point
is sealed inside the God below the ribs;
the second lifts a bitter sponge, oak-gall.

The maker's skilled hands raised all this
to the light and have let no-one leave
to flit to heaven or hell, to march
back into barracks and a night of wine.

Till this world burns and falls, they'll watch
that worn-down face, hear nothing from
the never-opened, slowly erasing lips.

The Man in the Pub Said

You see it more as you get old and stale
when memory's the dog and life the tail.

You see much clearer how it is, the norm
as death comes closer, rigour getting warm.

Stark as a streaker, factual as a fuck,
there's no denying it, no nip and tuck

can pluck it from the flesh, exit its grip,
no way you can jam-then-unjam its zip.

Your vision's tested, two dead rings for Dante,
straight as a Boro street, taut as a twisted panty,

as finely focused as a photo shoot,
sharper than any Moss Bros wedding suit.

Ruder than rude health, brassier than brass,
sharp and as splintered as a fist of glass:

your generation's risen, falls like grass
and like the rest you'll end tip under ass.

February

The young year's bent already with our sorrows,
manna of winter, startled whites of eyes.
A god giving bread can terrify.
The indifferent mercy of weather
showing its pale hand, saying 'Who?'
I don't know in truth, but it will melt
in its own mouth the fragile crystals
so crocodiles of tears will jam the becks,
rip chops off the leathery fells.

Grains of ice bounce on sandstone flags,
robin, wren, blackbird beak and claw
the peanut scraps shot down from aerial devilment,
that squadron screech of blue tits fighting
for all our lives through the bright flak.

Enquiry

What shall we do with all this love?
Nearing the end, not so far from the start
and this heap of love blocking the way,
obstacle to our tidy disposal of will.

Contemplate the spill from shopping bags,
suitcases, the most fond trash of it,
presents half-wrapped, half-opened.
Our correspondence grown considerate -

while still out there in a waste of water
the island of staring in fear the other vanishes,
though we've not disappeared, nor our accumulation.
Each can see through to the empty sea,

unfinished sky. By these I'll attest,
attempt my answer. All this heap of love,
a fall and sweeping together of snow,
its feathers plucked and brushed on a cold page.

How we badgered at, found hands
covered in it, eyes trading its soft blindness,
mouths stuffed with longing, patience
that against all weather denies death.

Hold breath its moment before melting -
then, as unwilling we drag down
into care and confusion, yell
its imagining, its ridiculous beauty.

Or you might shovel up after, root through
my late night leavings on what won't
follow. First hammer your chilly fingers in
the treacherous flesh we have not done with yet.

Remains

Wind, wet and white stuff
flattened the roadside grass.
This skeleton's unstitched, picked clean
so disassembled pelvis, scapulae, the rest
signal the compass points
on rusty green, rough of an old man's chin.

A week after snowfall the bones of it
anatomise the fell with dazzling lines of wall,
in drifted ossuaries down miry pits.
Shorn early of its storm-proof coat
this upland ewe, broad-backed,
shivers for birth and its crumb of summer.

I set the delicately nosing skull
as lookout on an edge of stone:
one pale card played
on stacks of blood-red tropic sand
a million icy winters steadied down.

Old Friend

Good morning. So another day. We'll take it.
Temperate with a light wind
teasing the skeins of cloud across the sun.

You've got to grips with my dark-humoured fun
and come to understand that what's beneath's
a sense, in every thing's delight, in ours,

of its sweet brevity. My dad, two years
my senior, might have glimpsed
that sooty nonconformist flare

but never was allowed to get that near,
barred by his wanting me to be the best,
the most he then could never make.

Mum used to say 'For heaven's sake'
hoping we'd just be happy, fit and fed.
She got through life never expecting much

but you have got a different touch,
accepting stoic, striving epicure,
young in the sixties, in your sixties young,

responding newborn as a Schubert song
to every pleasure, every injury.
From you I've learned to open up my heart,

managed to slow my slide into old fart,
to celebrate the better, weigh the worse
as with the kids whose photographs we show,

bright upstarts who already know,
as grandchildren will soon, we got it wrong
and they can do things better come what may.

For me and you is what remains to say
when luck has brought us here for one more day:
Good morning. Weather, sunlight, us. We'll take it.

Resolution

I am drowning the pack of them,
clubbing them over the side.
Long and short, coarse and learned,
adverbs, adjectives, just riddance.

Even one briefly or most solitary
gets their hymn humming, they all join
the chant down the lurid aisle
brightly as hues of their vestments.

Such veneration of particulars
I can do without, even the bare
cold empty, the bleakly.
God. Indescribable. Being or not being.

Lost Child

You were never a lost child,
always you held your hand
out to my hold. Smiled always
when I wrapped it round.

Never a lost child. You were
here all the day. All the night
you lay in your deep bed, floated
through walls into dreams.

Lost, you were never
a lost child, were you?
Fact is that I'll be one.
Gone away, the street all empty.

You will call me, call me.
To tea, to my favourite programme.
Bedtime. I still won't come. Never.
Again and again. A lost child.

Old Wolves

He woan't be baack for maany a year
So sheeep, sheeep, come out of theer
as Granddad Wolf sneaked in from Manchester
on the Number 26, snarkled past chapel and basket works,
used special key, slithered his scratchy claws
through shop, behind the counter, into the kitchen
and opened wide his mouth and eyes of Grandson Sheep,
me, who got out of theer and hid behind the sofa
or the pantry curtain. How they laughed afterwards,
lamb, really, and rheumatic, dentured wolf, whose jaws
grinned all night by the sink, in a chipped mug.

Now I am old, I get the canine part. A threat
to fleecy grandchildren, I send them scattering
through larger rooms, round backs of smarter furniture.
Now I know the trick, never to go to Manchester
but lurk, pretend a pensioner's ferocity.
Slyly I put on wolfskin, top hat, silk gloves,
white-spots-on-crimson pocket handkercher,
could pass quite unremarked across St. Peter's Square.
The mirror in the hall – ooh look at you now,
if it's not Granddad Wolf, to the life, back from the dead
of understairs. Not easy to shrug off.

In there the lambs are dancing in the light
waiting which door will open. I tell my old man in the glass,
my cue. He nods and will come too, the game's duplicitous.
We are and so are they, can play their parts. They run the show,
plot their determination, audition for the cast, treat me
as firm as Peter Quince would Bottom. So today
I'm a good wolf and must negotiate when bad ones come
to snatch my little deer from their frail house.
I hurl spells, utter threats, seduce with plastic burgers.
But in they tramp again, this time, I'm told,
their king leading the pack. Flashing his teeth and tie.

Beyond the wisdom of grandfathers, past the experience
of reformed carnivores who play at bites and snarls,
whose scratch is ticklish. The king of the bad wolves,
that war-crime-splattered general, defies us all.
Good, good-for-not-much wolf tells useless truth, I don't
know what to do. But four-years piglet does, will twirl
this story's devil by its bushed-out tail.
Tells me – Don't worry, Grandpa, it will be OK,
I will be Spiderman, you will be Batman, we will beat them.
As at last we do - with leaps and bounds, in expelled breaths,
by sharp karate chops. This once his generation is secured.

And mine - like any wolf with eyes long weighed with ice
or grandparent blessed with time's miracle,
our helpless babies grown to fullness, fuller still,
themselves the parents of these new-born lambs
that leap and totter – my generation starts its shrivelling,
its shadow tracing out from Manchester
across the web of airlines' arcing paths. There's one
lifts me from memory to Madrid, September, afternoon
where grandson gives this master-class for me,
the high-kick dance, the bonehouse-shattering cry.
Old wolves can learn new tricks, so young beasts thrive.

Equinoctial

For Ellie, 29 March 2006

Wind from the south west bearing rain
on its warm air; birds in the garden
clamour in mating, most coupled, some still
and unsolved in tag-wrestle threesomes.

We are waiting on time as our lives all do,
on the light's turn, a birth, some celebration
or acknowledgement. The gusts tug at our house
and lay daffodil heads, chase old leaves and wrappers.

These least, like your primed cards in their packs,
try on a bright dress, as one sliver of sun
glosses puddles. The odds stack for localised flooding,
not here though, east of Pennine embankments.

West of that watershed, becks add to rivers
carving again in Lune's snare-shifty sandflats
the names of the drowned that might sound so alike,
who now only wait with each tide in its coming

and bend with the moon through its barren seasons.
Here to the east, the older folk sleeping and just
before dawn, a flooding of life under night's hard stare.
Your child's born, sweet as air, sweet as rain, as spring.

Notes to the poems

Winter Breaks
Based around the twenty-four poems by Wilhelm Müller, which Franz Schubert took as the lyrics of his song cycle, *Winterreise*. Müller's anonymous wanderer is a young man rejected in love, an outcast tramping through winter landscapes which provide a plenitude of images to mirror his emotional and psychological states. The *Winter Breaks* isolate, also nameless, is much older. His winter, partly that of age, has its own contemporary qualities and is also informed by his familiarity with the Schubert songs and their young protagonist, whom he disparagingly calls Brokenheart. Other myths intrude and mingle in this older, later and more curmudgeonly (his word) head. Like Müller's 'Brokenheart', he converses with himself and at times addresses a lost or absent or distanced lover. The epigraphs are taken from the author's English versions of the German lyrics.

Tomb Decoration: Cattle
From the British Museum.

Song for Mario
Written in response to the Michael Radford film *Il Postino*.

The Afternoon Slot
Many Teesside writers benefited from creative writing courses held at Leeds University's Harrow Road Adult Education Centre in Middlesbrough. The Centre, axed by the University a few years ago in order to cut spending on non-essentials like lifelong learning, has since shared the fate of much local industrial plant: demolition.